GENDER AND FOOD INSECURITY IN SOUTHERN AFRICAN CITIES

BELINDA DODSON, ASIYATI CHIWEZA
AND LIAM RILEY

SERIES EDITOR: PROF. JONATHAN CRUSH

ACKNOWLEDGEMENTS

The following members of the AFSUN network coordinated the implementation of the survey on which this report is based: Ben Acquah, Jane Battersby-Lennard, Eugenio Bras, Jonathan Crush, Tebego Dlamini, Bruce Frayne, Trevor Hill, Florian Kroll, Clement Leduka, Chileshe Mulenga, Aloysius Mosha, Peter Mvula, Ndeyapo Nickanor, Wade Pendleton, Akiser Pomuti, Ines Raimundo, Michael Rudolph, Shaun Ruysenaar, Christa Schier, Nomcebo Simelane, Daniel Tevera, Maxton Tsoka, Godfrey Tawodzera and Percy Toriro. Cassandra Eberhardt and Maria Salamone provided technical and editorial assistance.

The financial support of the CIDA UPCD Tier One Program is gratefully acknowledged.

© AFSUN 2012

Published by the African Food Security Urban Network (AFSUN)
African Centre for Cities, University of Cape Town, Private Bag X3
Rondebosch 7701, South Africa; and
Southern African Research Centre, Queen's University,
152 Albert Street, Kingston, ON K7L 3N6, Canada
www.afsun.org

First published 2012

ISBN 978-1-920597-02-3

Cover photograph by Jonathan Crush. *Maputo market trader selling chickens from Brazil*

Production by Bronwen Müller, Cape Town

AUTHORS

Belinda Dodson is an Associate Professor in the Department of Geography at the University of Western Ontario.

Asiyati Chiweza is a Senior Lecturer in the Department of Political and Administrative Studies, Chancellor College, University of Malawi.

Liam Riley is a doctoral candidate in the Department of Geography at the University of Western Ontario.

Previous Publications in the AFSUN Series

CONTENTS

TABLES

FIGURES

1. INTRODUCTION

Sub-Saharan Africa has the fastest rate of urbanization of any region in the world and the highest proportion of under-nourished people.[1] These facts alone should make urban food security a high research and policy priority, but the reality is that policy discourse on food security in Africa is still largely focused on how to increase food production by providing agricultural inputs to smallholder farmers in rural areas.[2] This is despite a significant shift in the academic understanding of food security. In the years following the publication of Amartya Sen's book *Poverty and Famines* in 1981, increased attention was paid by food security researchers to the importance of the accessibility of food, in both physical and socio-economic terms, over straightforward food availability.[3] In recent years, the pendulum has swung back again to a narrow policy focus on production and food availability. Yet Southern Africa, for one, routinely attains food self-sufficiency in aggregate terms. At the same time, hunger and under-nutrition are prevalent across the region, in both city and country-side, in what has been described as an "invisible crisis" of food insecurity.[4]

To understand the extent and determinants of this crisis, and to provide the evidence for policy-makers to address it, the African Food Security Urban Network (AFSUN) designed and conducted a survey in eleven cities in nine SADC countries in 2008 and 2009. The resultant database provides baseline information on the state of urban food insecurity in Southern Africa. Applying the same survey instrument at the same time in different cities across the region has allowed comparisons to be drawn between countries and, in the case of South Africa, between different cities in the same country.[5] The primary aim of the survey was to assess levels of food insecurity amongst poor urban households using a range of food security indicators. The survey also sought to examine the relationship between poverty and food insecurity, and to find out where and how the urban poor access food. In addition to food-specific questions, the survey collected a range of socio-demographic data on households and their members. Analysis of the food security data by geographic location as well as by various socio-demographic variables has highlighted the multiple dimensions and determinants of food insecurity including the intersection of global, regional, national, local and household-level factors.[6]

The particular focus of this paper is on the gender dimensions of urban food security that emerge from the AFSUN survey data. The paper begins with a background theoretical discussion of how gender acts as a fundamental determinant of food (in)security, not only in terms of differences between the access to food of individual men and women, but also of gender-differentiated roles and responsibilities in food production, trade, preparation and consumption. This makes gender analysis an important element in understanding not only individual but also household and community food security. The paper then discusses the methodology used in the AFSUN survey and summarizes the overall survey findings, identifying opportunities and constraints for a gender-based analysis. Subsequent sections present a gender analysis of the survey data, using both individual and household level data to determine gender-based differences in livelihoods and food security, especially between different household types (i.e. female-centred, male-centred, nuclear and extended). This discussion shows how a gender analysis can shed additional light on the overall survey findings, including explanations for some of the trends and patterns identified.

2. WHY GENDER MATTERS IN URBAN FOOD SECURITY

Sen's path-breaking analysis examined food security as a matter of entitlements: the bundle of assets, resources, relationships and livelihood strategies that people can employ to secure their daily food needs.[7] Introducing questions of entitlement and economic access to discussions of food security has three important consequences. Firstly, it moves beyond the food production side of the equation to encompass food consumption. Food insecurity is explained in terms of entitlement failure and deprivation and not merely production shortfalls or the logistics of distribution. Secondly, by bringing food accessibility and cost into the equation, economic, social and political factors are placed at the very centre of analysis. Thirdly, this approach re-scales and relocates the locus of understanding. Understanding food security in terms of access and entitlement requires moving beyond national-scale balance sheets of total food production and aggregate consumption, to the scale of individuals, households and communities. It also moves the debate away from rural areas, where most food is produced, to urban areas, where most of the world's population now lives and where the urban poor go hungry amidst the plenty of stacked supermarket shelves and bustling markets. As an earlier AFSUN report noted, "urban food security is not, and never has been, simply an issue of how much food is produced."[8]

Food entitlements vary depending on where and who you are. Who you are matters because individual demographic attributes such as age, gender, marital and family status combine with class, ethnicity and other axes of discrimination to enable or constrain the individual's means of acquiring food. This occurs through differential access to employment and income or determining who gets how much food on their plate at the family dinner table. Where you are matters too because these demographic categorizations and social stratifications vary from place to place and because of geographical variation in the means by which food can be acquired. Although there is some production of food in cities, most urban households obtain food through financial exchange, supplemented in the case of the poor by charity, food sharing, welfare provision or begging. Food security in urban areas is thus closely tied to income, livelihood security and social safety nets.[9] Urban food insecurity, as a corollary, is linked to poverty, livelihood precariousness and the absence of safety nets. Urban food insecurity has been described as "the greatest humanitarian problem of the century", a result of (a) the decline in formal safety nets and their replacement by individual, household and community responses; and (b) changes in urban livelihood strategies, which have become more insecure and precarious.[10]

The centrality of livelihood strategies, entitlements and safety nets and the consequent focus on individuals, households and forms of social organization necessarily means that gender and gender relations are crucial to understanding urban food security. Women have been described as "the key to food security" and yet women's access to food is commonly both lower and more precarious than men's.[11] The reasons for this vulnerability include institutionalized marginalization through discriminatory laws and regulations, exclusion from male-dominated occupations and livelihoods, women's limited role in decision-making over use of household resources, and social practices that saddle women with burdens of reproductive labour.

In many contexts, women's lower economic and social status is exacerbated by cultural norms that privilege men and boys over women and girls, including when it comes to intra-household food allocation.[12] Gender roles and inequalities also shape food security in the wider population, not just for women and girls.[13] In most places, it is women who bear primary responsibility for buying, cooking and serving food to their families, especially children. In addition to these domestic roles, women are also commonly producers, preparers and traders of food in the commercial sphere, especially in the informal sector. Men, on the other hand, tend to control formal private-sector or state-controlled urban food systems.[14] In many African countries, women have a high degree of involvement in urban agriculture.[15] Everywhere, women have to juggle multiple productive and reproductive roles, balancing the need to earn an income (or grow food) with the need to perform other domestic tasks such as cooking, cleaning and childcare. In addition, in the absence of formal safety nets, it is women who commonly come together to create informal safety nets of food-sharing, mutual assistance and credit groups.

Women are often, and increasingly, heads and/or primary breadwinners of urban households. Far from being unusual or aberrant, households in which there is no adult male member are increasingly common in Southern Africa, as in many parts of the developing world.[16] The simplistic assumption of a direct and inevitable link between female household headship and poverty has been largely discredited.[17] However, female headship has been linked to greater poverty in a number of studies in Southern Africa.[18] Even so, one cannot assume that this automatically implies greater food insecurity. Studies in West Africa, for example, have found that female household headship augments household food security, despite their lower incomes, with female heads prioritizing food in spending choices to a greater extent than male-headed households.[19] These same food-secure female-headed households still exhibited greater vulnerability to sudden income loss or price shocks, given the higher proportion of household budgets spent on food. There is very little research that examines gender as a determinant of food security in Southern Africa, but clearly poverty and income alone are not adequate explanations of food insecurity, and factors such as the gender of household headship and the gendered nature of occupational categories and livelihood strategies can also be important determinants.

The factors that determine an urban resident's nutritional status operate at a variety of different scales (Figure 1).[20] Almost every aspect represented in the chart has gender implications. Men and women are included in or excluded from particular systems of food production and exchange in different ways; for example, through discriminatory systems of land tenure, resource endowment, or access to credit and capital. Men and women also participate unevenly in the formal and informal sectors, have unequal incomes and market access, and exhibit different levels of engagement in rural, urban and home-based production of food. Where men and women cohabit in functional households, their roles can be complementary, diversifying income and food sources and dividing household labour, thereby spreading risk and enhancing household food security. Female-headed households, by contrast, are commonly restricted in their assets, resources, labour power and livelihood opportunities, and thus also in their food entitlement bundles. Of course, not all nuclear households conform to a model of mutuality and complementarity, and husbands (or wives) in such households may engage in behaviours that erode rather than strengthen household food security. Female-centred households nevertheless face particular constraints.

FIGURE 1: The Dimensions of Urban Food Security

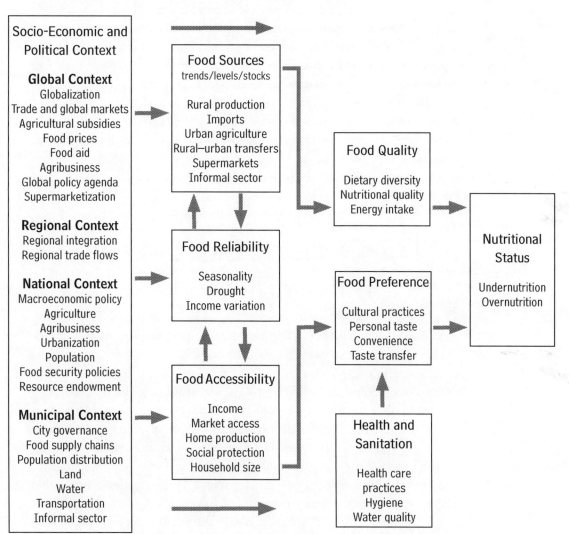

Source: Frayne et al. "The State of Urban Food Security in Southern Africa" adapted from Kennedy, "Food Security in the Context of Sub-Saharan Africa".

Moving across the flow chart to the household and individual scales, women's roles become even more central, and the squeeze faced by poorer households, especially those headed by women, becomes that much more apparent. Within a given household entitlement bundle, it is commonly women who purchase, prepare and allocate food to household members. Under more affluent circumstances, this responsibility might entail women doing the grocery shopping and the cooking; in less affluent circumstances, women are also expected to earn money to purchase food or to work to produce food. Female household heads have no choice but to combine productive and reproductive roles, limiting the time available for shopping and cooking and ensuring an adequate and nutritious diet for themselves and their families. Household composition, and not size alone, is thus an important determinant of food security, in combination with the occupation and income status of household members. Food preference and food quality also relate to gender, as social conventions can create gender differences in what foods people consume. Intra-household food allocation is not an egalitarian process, and in many households adult women are under-nourished relative to other household members.[21] Given the fundamental role of gender across the food system, gender analysis is essential to understanding food security in any context, but perhaps especially so in cities, where access to income is such a vital source of food entitlement.

3. THE OVERALL PICTURE OF FOOD INSECURITY

The AFSUN Urban Food Security Survey was conducted simultaneously in late 2008 and early 2009 in eleven cities in nine countries: Blantyre (Malawi), Cape Town (South Africa), Gaborone (Botswana), Harare (Zimbabwe), Johannesburg (South Africa), Lusaka (Zambia), Maputo (Mozambique), Manzini (Swaziland), Maseru (Lesotho), Msunduzi (South Africa) and Windhoek (Namibia). The surveyed cities "represent a mix of large and small cities; cities in crisis, in transition and those on a strong developmental path; and a range of local governance structures and capacities as well as natural environments."[22] They offer considerable scope for comparative analysis as well as the breadth required to capture the status of urban food security across the region. Key AFSUN survey findings are summarized in this section: firstly, to present an overall picture of urban food security and secondly, to highlight areas to which attention is paid in the subsequent gender analysis.

Details of the survey design and methodology may be found in an earlier report in this series.[23] The surveys drew their sample from poor urban neighbourhoods.[24] In larger cities, such as Cape Town and Johannesburg, more than one neighbourhood was selected, including a mix of formal and informal housing. Within the selected neighbourhoods, households were sampled using systematic random sampling. Household heads or other responsible adults answered a standardized questionnaire. The resulting AFSUN Urban Food Security Regional Database contains information on 6,453 households and 28,771 individuals.

One of the striking findings of the survey was the high level of diversity within and amongst cities. In this context, average or aggregate figures can be misleading, although generalization is still possible. An especially relevant finding for the purposes of gender analysis, for example, is the high proportion of female-centred households. Fully 34% of the households surveyed were female-centred, slightly more than "conventional" nuclear households at 32% (Table 1).[25] The proportion ranged from a low of 19% in Blantyre to a high of 53% in Msunduzi, although the proportion was over 30% in seven of the eleven cities.

TABLE 1: Household Types by City											
	Wind-hoek	Gabo-rone	Maseru	Manzini	Maputo	Blan-tyre	Lusaka	Harare	Cape Town	Msun-duzi	Johann-esburg	Total
Female-Centred (%)	33	47	38	38	27	19	20	23	42	53	33	34
Male-Centred (%)	21	23	10	17	8	6	3	7	11	12	16	12
Nuclear (%)	23	20	35	32	21	41	48	37	34	22	36	32
Extended (%)	24	8	17	12	45	34	28	33	14	13	15	22
N	448	399	802	500	397	432	400	462	1,060	556	996	6,452

In addition to a large number of female-centred households, 5% of extended and 5% of nuclear households were headed by women (Table 2). This means that female-centred should not be conflated with female-headed, as even households with a husband or male partner were sometimes described as female-headed. Although the survey did not enquire into the specific circumstances of such female-headed nuclear and extended households, they might be households where a male household head is a migrant who is not always present, leaving a female as de facto household head. The gender analysis in this paper (Sections 4 to 9) is focused primarily on female-centred households, drawing comparisons between these and other household types.

TABLE 2: Household Type by Sex of Household Head						
	Male		Female		Total for HH Type	
	N	%	N	%	Male %	Female %
Female-Centred	0	0	2,263	93	0	100
Male-Centred	795	20	0	0	100	0
Nuclear	1,979	50	102	4	95	5
Extended	1,222	31	69	3	95	5
Total	3,996	100	2,434	100		

Given that the survey respondents were drawn specifically from poorer urban neighbourhoods, the high incidence of female-centred households already hints that there may be an association between female-centredness and urban poverty. This was borne out in subsequent gender-based analysis of income and other socio-economic variables (see Section 5 below). The predominance of women in the sampled poor neighbourhoods is reinforced by the individual sex data, which showed an imbalance of 54% females and 46% males. Again with the exception of Blantyre, which had a 50:50 sex-ratio, all of the neighbourhoods surveyed had more women than men. The survey sample was also young, with 32% being aged 0-15, only 4% aged 60 and above and fully 75% being under the age of 35. Household size, however, was relatively small at an average of five, although with a wide range (1 to 21). The average household size in individual cities ranged from three in Gaborone to seven in Maputo. Another important finding, indicative of high rates of urbanization in the region, was that 38% of the surveyed households were "migrant" households, comprised entirely of members who had been born somewhere other than the city in which the survey took place. Almost 50% were "mixed" households of migrant and non-migrant members and only 13% of the households surveyed consisted of members who had all been born in the city.

Overall, then, the sample showed high dependency ratios, high levels of female headship, considerable in-migration to the surveyed cities, and disproportionate numbers of women and children in poorer neighbourhoods. Findings also indicated high levels of poverty and vulnerability. High unemployment levels were evident in reported sources of income, with only one-third of total household income coming from wage work. Casual employment accounted for another 16%, social grants 13% and informal sector activity 10% of total income. Poverty was also evident in the high proportion of (already meagre) household income spent on food: almost 50% of the reported household expenditure went on food, reaching a high of 62% in Harare and over 40% in all cities except Windhoek (36%).[26]

Where food has to be purchased, income poverty is a significant determinant of food insecurity. Across the AFSUN sample, food purchases were the predominant food source, despite the multiple strategies and sources drawn upon to fill the household food basket. Food was purchased mainly from supermarkets (80% of households), informal vendors (70%) and small outlets such as corner stores, take-away restaurants and fast-food outlets (68%). In terms of the frequency of food purchases, the most frequent sources were informal markets and street vendors, visited daily by

31% of households: "the heavy use of ad hoc sources of food on a regular, almost daily basis is consistent with the behaviour of people with limited income."[27] Borrowing food from others, sharing meals with neighbours and growing food for household consumption were all reported as food sources by approximately one-fifth of households. Over one quarter (28%) reported receiving food transfers from outside the city, which could include remittances from migrant household members, food from family members or social networks in rural areas.

Food insecurity was measured using four composite indicators: The Household Food Insecurity Access Scale (HFIAS), Household Food Insecurity Access Prevalence Indicator (HFIAP), Household Dietary Diversity Scale (HDDS) and Months of Adequate Household Provisioning Indicator (MAHFP):

- **HFIAS**: The HFIAS score is a continuous measure of the degrees of food insecurity (access) in the household in the month prior to the survey.[28] An HFIAS score is calculated for each household based on answers to nine 'frequency-of-occurrence' questions. The minimum score is 0 and the maximum is 27. The higher the score, the more food insecurity (access) the household experienced. The lower the score, the less food insecurity (access) a household experienced.

- **HFIAP**: This indicator categorizes households into four levels of household food insecurity (access): food secure, and mild, moderately and severely food insecure.[29] Households are categorized as increasingly food insecure as they respond affirmatively to more severe conditions and/or experience those conditions more frequently.

- **HDDS**: Dietary diversity refers to how many food groups are consumed within the household over a given period.[30] The maximum number, based on the FAO (UN Food and Agriculture Organization) classification of food groups for Africa, is 12. An increase in the average number of food groups consumed provides a quantifiable measure of improved household food access. In general, any increase in the dietary diversity reflects an improvement in the household's diet.

- **MAHFP**: The MAHFP indicator captures changes in the household's ability to ensure that food is available above a minimum level the year round.[31] Households are asked to identify in which months (during the past 12 months) they did not have access to sufficient food to meet their household needs.

All four indicators revealed widespread food insecurity in the overall AFSUN sample. On the HFIAS scale of 0 (no food insecurity) to 27 (high food insecurity), the average household score was 10. The average was skewed by Johannesburg's relatively low score of 4.7, with eight of the eleven cities recording scores of over 10. The HFIAS was highest in Harare and Manzini, each with a score close to 15. When taken in conjunction with the HFIAP indicator – which categorizes households as food secure or mildly, moderately or severely food insecure – the extent and intensity of food insecurity becomes even more evident. Combining moderately and severely food insecure categories into a single "food insecure" category revealed that 76% of households did not have enough to eat. In Manzini, Maseru, Harare and Lusaka, the figure was over 90%. Even in relatively affluent South Africa, Cape Town and Msunduzi showed higher than average levels of food insecurity, at 80% and 87% of households respectively. Blantyre, which by other indicators was relatively poor, recorded a much lower level of food insecurity, at only 51%.[32] Food insecure households also recorded significantly lower dietary diversity than food secure households, suggesting nutritionally inadequate diets in terms of both quantity and quality of food. Months of adequate food provisioning further demonstrated the extent of food insecurity, with households classified as food insecure on the HSIAP score also going without adequate food for, on average, four months of the year.

The survey found a statistically significant relationship between food insecurity and poverty. The correlation of food security with income across all household types was especially strong, demonstrating the importance of a reliable cash income to enable households to purchase food. There was also a correlation with employment status, although this was less strong. Casual work in particular was associated with food insecure households, but even wage work was no guarantee of food security. Education too was correlated with food security, being linked to better employment status and higher incomes.

There was a striking difference between food secure and food insecure households in terms of where they purchased food. For food secure households, the top-ranked sources were supermarkets, small shops and take-aways, and then informal markets and street food. For food insecure households, the ranking was reversed: first were informal market and street food sources, second small shops and take-aways, and third supermarkets. Lack of transportation and the need to buy small amounts of food on a daily basis, and at locations close to home, are likely explanations for why members of poorer households choose these less formal, but not necessarily cheaper, food sources. Food insecure households were also considerably more sensitive to price hikes, with 92% of food insecure households reporting that they had had to go without food in the previous six months, compared to 38% of food secure households. Borrowing from or sharing food with neighbours, receiving food transfers (e.g. from family in rural areas) and practising urban agriculture were all more common amongst food insecure households.

The original report on the survey results described the statistical relationship between household type and food security as being "surprisingly weak."[33] The report also concluded that "food security has a gender dimension to it, with female-centred households the most insecure (although by a small proportion)."[34] This raises a number of questions. What is it about households with no male partner that makes them more likely to be food insecure? Is it simply that they are headed by a single adult, or are there particular factors associated with women as household heads that make them especially vulnerable? How does female-centredness relate to the income, employment and education variables that proved significant in the overall findings on urban food security in the region? Is there any evidence of female-centred households spending a higher proportion of their incomes on food, and prioritizing food over other expenditure? Do female-centred households obtain their food from the same sources as other household types, and does this make them more or less vulnerable to price or other shocks? Do female-centred households rank differently than other household types in each of the four food security indicators? While the AFSUN data does not allow us to answer all of these questions, a breakdown of the survey data by gender (for individual variables such as education and occupation) and by household type (for household-level variables such as income and poverty indices) offers important insights into the role of gender as a factor in urban food security.

While true in the aggregate, the finding that female-centred households are only slightly over-represented in the "food insecure" category is to some extent a product of the process of combining four food security categories into just two (secure/insecure). Unfortunately, this conceals the fact that the gender-based differential is more marked, especially if one looks only at the "severely food insecure" category. Geographical aggregation also masks significant variation by city in the levels of food security in different household types, as the proportions of female-centred households are not the same in each city. As discussed in the detailed gender analysis below, further interrogation of the survey findings along these lines suggests that gender and household type are more significant than originally thought.

The survey data provide challenges and opportunities for conducting a gender analysis. Both individual and household level data were collected, which allows comparison of socio-demographic data on household and individual bases, and linkage of individual characteristics to household food security outcomes. The detailed gender analysis that follows frequently compares female-centred households to nuclear households, which were roughly equally represented in the survey at about one-third each of the total number of households. The nuclear household certainly cannot be considered to be the "standard" form in this region, giving particular relevance and urgency to understanding food security in female-centred households. Although household-level analysis yielded interesting and important findings, it was inherently limiting in terms of understanding intra-household differences amongst individuals, as household level figures for food security might mask hidden gender-based hunger. The findings presented below therefore represent a foundation for further analysis, which would need to include both qualitative research and further "unpacking" of the household to understand more fully, not merely the intersection but the integration of gender with other determinants of urban food security.

4. DEMOGRAPHIC COMPARISON OF HOUSEHOLD TYPES

This section breaks down household demographic data by gender, examining the age distribution within each household type, the relative size of different household types and the education levels of household heads. This breakdown identifies key socio-demographic differences between household types and provides insights into the gender dynamics underpinning differential household food insecurity (see Section 8 below).

4.1 Age Distribution and Household Type

One plausible hypothesis is that female-centred households have higher dependency ratios, with a higher proportion of children to adults, and that this might undermine household food security. A comparison of the age distribution within each household type, however, reveals that female-centred households closely resemble nuclear and extended households (Figure 2). Male-centred households (i.e. households without a female spouse or partner) are actually more distinctive. As expected, children are more commonly found with their mothers than their fathers in single-parent households. There were also more people aged 70 or older in female-centred households than in any other types of household (3%, compared to 1% for nuclear households and 2% for extended and male-centred households). Using the conventional definition of "dependant" as children under 15 and adults 65 and over, the dependency ratio in both female-centred and nuclear households is 59%, while in male-centred households it is much lower at only 25%. This means that any difference in food security status between female-centred and nuclear households cannot be attributed to higher dependency ratios.

FIGURE 2: Age Distribution by Household Type

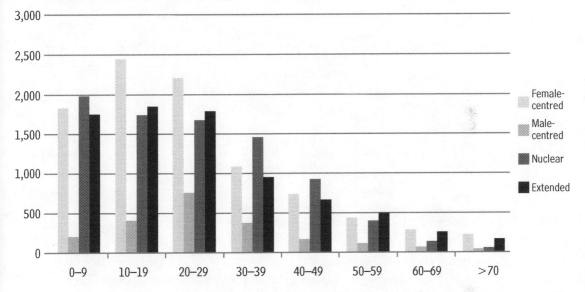

The main age differences between female-centred and other household types are found in the adult age categories. Female-centred households, along with extended households, have more members in the younger, 15-29 age brackets (38%) than nuclear households (30%). Nuclear households have relatively more members in the 30-49 categories than any other household type, whereas male-centred households are particularly over-represented in the young adult, 20-34 age cohorts. These patterns suggest that young adults, even those with children, are remaining unmarried, with young women either staying in extended family households or forming female-centred households without a male partner. The fact that these young women commonly have child dependants affects their ability to pursue education opportunities or engage fully in remunerative occupations. Age and parental status thus intersect with gender, so that any differences between female-centred and other household types cannot be attributed to gender alone.

4.2 Household Size and Type

Household size is an important factor in household food security as more people require more food, although food needs and consumption vary by age and gender.[35] Not surprisingly, extended households are by far the largest, with 6% having more than 10 members and the majority, 53%, having 6-10 members (Table 3). Amongst the remaining household types, female-centred households are the largest, with 2% of female-centred households having more than 10 members and 22% having 6-10 members. No nuclear household has more than 10 members and 82% of nuclear households have only 1-5 members. Male-centred households are the smallest, with 89% comprising five people or fewer.

TABLE 3: Household Size by Household Type				
Size	Female-Centred Households %	Male-Centred Households %	Nuclear Households %	Extended Households %	All Households %
1–5	76	89	82	42	73
6–10	22	10	18	53	25
>10	2	1	0	6	2
Total	100	100	100	100	100

There is a high level of geographic diversity in the sample. Maseru and Harare, for example, are at opposite ends of the spectrum of difference between female-centred and nuclear households (Table 4). In Harare, 6% of female-centred households have 10 or more members whereas no nuclear households are this large. Female-centred households are even more likely than extended families (4%) to have 10 or more members and are far larger than male-centred and nuclear households. At the opposite extreme is Maseru, where female-centred households and nuclear households have the same proportion of households in each size category.

TABLE 4: Household Size by Household Type: Maseru and Harare					
		Female-Centred Households (N=305) %	Male-Centred Households (N=80) %	Nuclear Households (N=281) %	Extended Households (N=136) %	All Households (N=802) %
Maseru	1–5	84	89	84	59	80
	6–10	16	11	16	38	19
	>10	0	0	0	4	1
	Total	100	100	100	100	100
		Female-Centred Households (N=106) %	Male-Centred Households (N=32) %	Nuclear Households (N=171) %	Extended Households (N=153) %	All Households (N=462) %
Harare	1–5	53	69	73	35	56
	6–10	42	31	27	61	42
	>10	6	0	0	4	2
	Total	100	100	100	100	100

Although the initial report on the AFSUN findings found that overall the correlation between household size and food security was statistically insignificant, in those cities where female-centred households are significantly larger, variation in household size, in conjunction with income, is potentially important as an explanatory factor.[36] Female-centred households are, by definition, headed by women. They are less likely to have multiple income earners, and those that are income earners are likely to earn less than men (as is borne out in the socio-economic analysis below). Hence their larger household size implies a likelihood of higher food insecurity, as lower income has to be divided amongst more people, reducing per capita food expenditure. These more complex relationships are not explored here, but warrant further exploration in future, multivariate analysis of the AFSUN data.

4.3 Education of Household Head

The level of education of the household head has an important bearing on the socio-economic status and income security of households, and thus also on their food security. More than half (51%) of the heads of female-centred households have only primary education or no formal schooling (Table 5). Amongst heads of nuclear households, almost all of whom are men, 61% have a high school or post-secondary education, with 39% having only primary or no formal education. Heads of extended and male-centred households fall in between but still with a majority having a high school education or higher. These results reflect women's marginalization from the formal education system and the difficulties they face in attaining higher education in particular. This in turn contributes to their lower income earning potential and higher vulnerability to food insecurity.

TABLE 5: Level of Education of Household Head by Household Type				
	Female-Centred Households %	Male-Centred Households %	Nuclear Households %	Extended Households %
No formal schooling	11	9	7	8
Primary school	40	32	32	36
High school	41	45	51	43
Tertiary education	7	14	10	13
Total	100	100	100	100

The effects of education on household food security go beyond occupational and income earning implications. Education, especially of females, is a significant predictor of household food security, as educated women and girls are better equipped to care for their families and prepare nutritious meals.[37] The finding of lower education levels of heads of female-centred households is thus likely to be an important explanatory factor in terms of both food and nutrition security.

5. ECONOMIC PROFILE OF DIFFERENT HOUSEHOLD TYPES

5.1 Income and Household Type

Female-centred households are at a disadvantage in terms of income. A comparison of absolute income figures in the region would be fraught with difficulty due to widely varying national economies, currency conversion issues and different costs of living. Income terciles were therefore calculated for each city individually and then aggregated so as to reflect relative poverty rather than absolute poverty. The difference in household income by household type is apparent in the income terciles. If household type was not an influencing factor, then each household type would have one third of its total number in each income tercile.

Female-centred households are by far the most likely to fall into the "poorest" tercile, with 41% of female-centred households in this category (Table 6). Female-centred households also have the smallest proportion in the "least poor" category. Best off were extended households, who were most likely to be in the "least poor" tercile. This probably reflects the higher number of adult income earners in these households and also the higher levels of education of their household heads. Nuclear households came second and male-centred households third in this tercile-based ranking of household income. Had these calculations been done on a per capita basis, the relative poverty of female-centred households would have been even more evident, given their larger household size.

TABLE 6: Household Income Terciles by Household Type			
	Female-Centred Households %	Male-Centred Households %	Nuclear Households %	Extended Households %
Poorest	41	33	26	22
Less poor	32	36	36	20
Least poor	27	31	38	48
Total	100	100	100	100

Although extended households are even larger, they also earn significantly more income. Female-centred households, with their evident income disadvantage, would certainly be expected to experience significantly higher levels of food insecurity.

5.2 Sources of Household Income by Household Type

Many households earn income from more than one source (Table 7). The high incidence of multiple, if insecure, sources of income holds for all household types, but is especially prevalent amongst female-centred households. This does not translate into higher income for female-centred households; rather, it suggests the need to draw on multiple sources of income to make ends meet.

Several important differences are apparent between female-centred and other household types in terms of income sources. Firstly, far fewer female-centred households (43%) reported any income from wage work (compared to 56% of extended households, 57% of male-centred households and 60% of nuclear households). Secondly, female-centred households are slightly more likely to earn income from rent than any of the other household types. Thirdly, female-centred households are significantly more likely to receive income from social grants (31% of households compared to 15% of nuclear households). Social grants (in the form of child grants, pensions and other forms of state-provided welfare) are most prevalent in the three South African cities. Fourthly, female-centred households are more likely to receive cash remittances from other areas.

There were also some striking similarities. Casual work and informal business are important income sources across all household types, and the proportion of female-centred households earning income from these sources is not significantly different from other types of household. Very few households in any category earned income from the sale of urban agricultural produce. Overall, however, amongst a generally poor and vulnerable population, female-centred households appear to be more economically precarious than other household types.

TABLE 7: Sources of Urban Household Income by Household Type					
	Female-Centred Households %	Male-Centred Households %	Nuclear Households %	Extended Households %	All Households %
Wage work	43	57	60	56	53
Social grants	31	10	15	16	20
Casual work	25	23	28	21	25
Informal business	14	10	16	18	15
Remittances	12	7	6	8	9
Rent	8	5	5	6	6
Formal business	3	3	4	6	4
Rural farm products	2	1	2	3	2
Urban farm products	2	0	2	4	2
Gifts	2	2	1	2	2
Aid (cash)	1	0	1	0	0
Aid (vouchers)	0	1	0	0	0
Other sources	3	3	1	2	2
Note: Multiple responses allowed					

5.3 Gender and Occupation

Differences in levels and sources of income in large part reflect gender differences in occupation. Twenty-two percent of all men and 30% of women fall into the category of "unemployed" or "job seeking" (Table 8). The most common occupation for women is unremunerated house-work, given as their primary occupation by 12%. Scholar or student is the main occupation of 11% of men and 9% of women, with mostly older youths still in high school. Adding these three categories together, it means that more than half of the women in the sample are engaged primarily in unremunerated activity. By comparison, the percentage of men in a similar position is just over one-third (34%).

The most common paid activity for women in these cities is domestic service (still only 7% of the female sample) followed by trading, hawking or vending (at 6%). Thus, even women's remunerative activities are in insecure and precarious occupations. Men fare little better, with their most common occupation being manual labour (17%), predominantly "unskilled" (9%). A few women (6%) are engaged in manual labour, and indeed throughout the occupation profile there is a clear gendering of labour sectors. Women are more likely than men to be teachers or health workers, and men more likely than women to be in the police, military or security sector. Men are also twice as likely as women to be professional workers (4% versus 2%), although these occupations are generally uncommon in this sample of people from poorer urban neighbourhoods.

TABLE 8: Most Common Occupations of Adults by Gender								
Men's Occupations				Women's Occupations				
Rank		N	%	Rank		N	%
1.	Unemployed/ Job seeker	1,587	22	1.	Unemployed/ Job seeker	2,708	30
2.	Scholar/Student	814	11	2.	Housework (unpaid)	1,067	12
3.	Unskilled manual	660	9	3.	Scholar/Student	834	9
4.	Skilled manual	582	8	4.	Domestic worker	679	7
5.	Service worker	503	7	5.	Trader/Hawker/ Vendor	573	6
6.	Own business	421	6	6.	Own business	566	6
7.	Security personnel	371	5	7.	Pensioner	485	5
8.	Pensioner	286	4	8.	Service worker	382	4
9.	Professional worker	277	4	9.	Unskilled manual	353	4
10.	Trader/Hawker/ Vendor	250	3	10.	Other	229	3
11.	Other	231	3	11.	Office worker	185	2
12.	Truck driver	226	3	12.	Skilled manual worker	148	2
13.	Civil servant	147	2	13.	Professional worker	141	2
14.	Office worker	123	2	14.	Teacher	136	1
15.	Police/Military	100	1	15.	Health worker	115	1
16.	Foreman	99	1	16.	Managerial office	88	1
17.	Teacher	95	1	17.	Farmer	85	1
18.	Managerial office	94	1	18.	Security personnel	78	1
19.	Domestic worker	89	1	19.	Informal producer	70	1
20.	Mine worker	81	1	20.	Civil servant	69	1
21.	Housework (unpaid)	55	1	21.	Employer/manager	47	1
22.	Farmwork (paid)	48	1	22.	Police/military	28	<1
23.	Informal producer	47	1	23.	Farmwork (unpaid)	18	<1
24.	Employer/manager	47	1	24.	Farmwork (paid)	16	<1
25.	Farmer	42	1	25.	Truck driver	8	<1
26.	Health worker	33	<1	26.	Mine worker	6	<1
27.	Fisherman	19	<1	27.	Foreman	4	<1
28.	Farmwork (unpaid)	16	<1	28.	Fisherman	4	<1
Total		7,343	100	Total		9,122	100

The weaker position of women individually contributes to the weaker position of female-centred households, although the occupational profile is also indicative of broader vulnerability in the context of widespread under-employment. The common definition of "dependency ratio" (assuming adults contribute to household income, with only children and the elderly being classified as dependants) is clearly inapplicable. In situations of urban poverty and limited employment opportunities, financial dependants are as likely to be adults.

5.4 Lived Poverty Index by Household Type

A useful measure of "lived poverty" is Afrobarometer's Lived Poverty Index (LPI).[38] The LPI is calculated based on how often people report being unable to secure a basket of basic necessities: food, clean water, medicine/medical treatment, cooking oil and cash income. Responses are grouped into a single index on a scale that ranges from 0 (never going without) to 4 (always going without), so that a higher value indicates more severe deprivation. The average LPI for all households in the survey was 1.1, although the scores varied from a high of 2.2 in Harare to a low of 0.6 in Johannesburg.

In the aggregate picture, female-centred households are only slightly worse off on the LPI than other household types (Table 9). Yet female-centred households have a higher LPI than nuclear households in every city with the exception of Johannesburg, where female-centred households actually recorded a lower LPI than any other household type. Other exceptions include Msunduzi, where male-centred households scored worse, and Manzini, where extended households and female-centred households had an equal LPI of 1.6.

The LPI range for female-centred households (from 2.3 in Harare to 0.5 in Johannesburg) is wider than the spread in the overall sample. Based on lived poverty, the worst place to be is therefore in a female-centred household in Harare, while the best place to be is in a female-centred household in Johannesburg. Maputo is the city with the biggest LPI gap between female-centred and other household types. The finding that female-centred households have a consistently higher LPI shows that they are more likely to go without basic necessities, including food; a situation that is linked to their lower incomes, higher unemployment and greater reliance on inconsistent income sources.

TABLE 9: Lived Poverty Index by Household Type					
	Female-Centred Households	Male-Centred Households	Nuclear Households	Extended Households	All Households
Windhoek	1.2	1.1	1.0	1.1	1.1
Gaborone	1.1	1.0	1.0	0.9	1.1
Maseru	1.5	1.3	1.4	1.4	1.4
Manzini	1.6	1.4	1.4	1.6	1.5
Maputo	1.3	1.0	1.0	1.0	1.1
Blantyre	1.1	0.7	0.9	0.8	0.9
Lusaka	1.6	1.1	1.4	1.4	1.5
Harare	2.3	2.1	2.2	2.1	2.2
Cape Town	1.1	1.1	1.0	0.8	1.0
Msunduzi	0.8	0.9	0.7	0.7	0.8
Johannesburg	0.5	0.7	0.6	0.7	0.6
Total	1.2	1.1	1.1	1.1	1.1

The three South African cities tend to have lower LPI scores than the other eight cities in the survey (Table 10). The biggest gap is amongst female-centred households: in South African cities their LPI is 0.8, whereas in cities outside South Africa it is nearly double at 1.5. This almost certainly reflects the impact of social grants, and especially child grants, in South Africa.[39]

TABLE 10: Lived Poverty Index by Household Type					
	Household structure				Total
	Female-Centred	Male-Centred	Nuclear	Extended	
Three SA cities	0.8	0.9	0.8	0.7	0.8
Cities outside SA	1.5	1.2	1.4	1.3	1.4
Total	1.2	1.1	1.1	1.1	1.1

6. FOOD PURCHASE AND HOUSEHOLD INCOME

When a high proportion of total household expenditure goes on food, this is widely recognized as an indicator of poverty and food insecurity. Not only does the immediate need to buy food outweigh long-term needs such as investment in education, business and housing, but there is little leeway in household budgets when they are subjected to income or price shocks. Households of all types in all eleven cities spend a considerable proportion of their income on food, with an average of just under 50% (Table 11). Windhoek was the lowest at 36% and Harare the highest at 62%. Household expenditure on food exceeded 50% in five cities including Harare (62%), Cape Town (55%), Lusaka (54%), Maputo (53%) and Msunduzi (52%).

TABLE 11: Food Purchases as Proportion of Household Expenditure					
	Female-Centred Households %	Male-Centred Households %	Nuclear Households %	Extended Households %	All Households %
Windhoek	37	36	35	36	36
Gaborone	48	41	44	50	46
Maseru	46	49	46	45	46
Manzini	42	42	43	43	42
Maputo	55	57	54	51	53
Blantyre	48	37	49	45	47
Lusaka	55	55	54	52	54
Harare	70	53	62	61	62
Cape Town	54	57	55	53	55
Msunduzi	53	56	48	53	52
Johannesburg	53	43	48	47	49
Total	51	46	50	49	50

Despite their lower income and higher LPI scores, female-centred households do not generally appear to spend a significantly greater proportion of their income on food than nuclear households (51% to 50%). However, geographical disaggregation again reveals considerable diversity. In five cities (Gaborone, Harare, Msunduzi, Johannesburg and Windhoek), female-centred households spend a higher share of their income on food than nuclear households. In the other six cities (Maseru, Manzini, Maputo, Blantyre, Lusaka and Cape Town), there is very little difference in the proportional expenditure on food by female-centred and nuclear households. The worst place of all to be by this measure is in a female-centred household in Harare, where almost 70% of household income went on food. The best is a nuclear household in Windhoek (at 35%).

Johannesburg, which appeared to fare better on the LPI score, does considerably less well in terms of proportional expenditure on food, suggesting a vulnerability to price or income shocks. Overall, the small differences in relative food expenditure between household types indicate the stretched budgets of almost all households, with little flexibility in expenditure. The fact that female-centred households had lower incomes does mean, however, that their absolute expenditure on food must be lower than that of other household types.

7. SOURCES OF FOOD

A central aim of the AFSUN survey was to understand how alternative food sources are used to access food and help sustain household food security in different household types (Table 12). Across all household types, supermarkets are used by the largest number of households, indicative of the penetration of supermarkets into the food retail sector in the region.[40] Female-centred and male-centred households are more likely than nuclear or extended households to buy food from supermarkets (79% of all households and 84% of male-centred and female-centred households reported supermarkets as a food source). Also revealing is the diversity of food sources for most households, including buying food from small shops, restaurants, take-aways, market stalls and street vendors, along with various social transfers such as remittances, sharing food and borrowing food from neighbours. Female-centred households are the least likely to get food from small outlets, which may be due to the higher costs of these sources and the relatively lower incomes of female-centred households. These kinds of sources were still used by approximately two-thirds of female-centred households, however.

Female-centred households recorded lower usage of informal markets and street vendors than either nuclear or extended households. It is difficult to identify an explanation for this, as these sources can be cheaper than supermarkets. In part, it could be a reflection of geographic variability, where cities in which extended households are more common are coincidentally those cities where informal markets and street foods are generally more accessible and popular. On the other hand, female-centred households are more prevalent in cities with readier access to supermarkets, such as those in South Africa.

Non-commercial sources include home-grown food, reported by 22% of households. Extended households are by far the most likely to grow food (29%), followed by nuclear households (24%), female-centred households (19%) and male-centred households (15%). This suggests that the availability of household labour is an important determinant of urban agriculture, with the larger size of extended households proving an advantage. Income is also necessary to purchase agricultural inputs, which may be a further obstacle for poorer households, along with limited access to land. Very few households of any type receive formal food transfers from sources such as food aid or community kitchens, although within this small proportion, female-centred households are most common.

TABLE 12: Household Sources of Food by Household Type				
	% of Households Using Source			
	Female-Centred Households	Male-Centred Households	Nuclear Households	Extended Households
Supermarket	84	84	76	69
Small shop/restaurant/ take away	65	69	70	69
Informal market/ street food	64	64	73	79
Food transfers from outside city	28	27	26	31
Borrow food from others	23	15	22	19
Sharing with neighbours/ other households	22	18	23	19
Food from neighbours/ other households	22	17	22	18
Urban agriculture	19	15	24	29
Remittances (food)	8	5	8	10
Community food kitchen	5	4	4	3
Food aid	3	2	2	2
Other source	2	1	2	2

More significant than any formal transfers are informal food transfers, such as sharing, borrowing or otherwise receiving food from neighbours. These transfers are a food source for roughly one-fifth of the surveyed households, including those in the female-centred and nuclear categories. Male-centred households are least likely to receive food from such sources, possibly an indication of lesser need but also perhaps a reflection of women's role in sustaining informal safety nets. Remittances of food are reported by a small but significant 8% of respondent households, again equally by female-centred and nuclear households and to a lesser extent by male-centred households. Overall, and especially for female-centred households, the picture is one of high dependence on commercial sources of food, especially supermarkets, and thus on cash income in order to purchase food. The necessity to supplement these sources by drawing on social capital in the form of various coping strategies is "characteristic of food-poor communities generally and pervasive in all of the cities surveyed" and across all household types.[41]

In the sample as a whole, 28% of households reported receiving food transfers from households living elsewhere (i.e. from outside their own city of residence, either another city or a rural area). Aggregated across all eleven cities, there does not appear to be much difference amongst household types: 28% of female-centred households, 26% of nuclear households and 31% of extended households. Yet the geographical variation in food transfers is considerable, from a low of 14% of households in Johannesburg to a high of 47% of households in Windhoek, with Lusaka and Harare also above 40% (Table 13). Furthermore, in eight of the eleven cities, more female-centred households than nuclear households reported receiving food transfers. In Johannesburg, for example, although the overall proportion of households receiving food transfers was low, more than twice as many female-centred households as nuclear households received such transfers. The proportions were equal in Maseru, but in both Lusaka and Gaborone, it was nuclear households rather than female-centred households that were more likely to receive food transfers. To explain this variability requires further analysis of social networks, migration patterns and family ties, but it does appear that in the majority of cities, food transfers are disproportionately important for female-centred households.

TABLE 13: Receipt of Food Transfers by Household Type				
	Female-Centred Households %	Male-Centred Households %	Nuclear Households %	Extended Households %	Total %
Windhoek	51	40	44	51	47
Gaborone	18	22	32	28	23
Maseru	36	35	36	42	37
Manzini	35	43	28	39	35
Maputo	24	30	18	17	20
Blantyre	40	44	32	37	36
Lusaka	32	25	52	41	44
Harare	51	33	38	42	42
Cape Town	20	15	14	22	18
Msunduzi	27	25	18	18	24
Johannesburg	18	19	8	15	14
Total	28	27	26	31	28

8. LEVELS OF FOOD INSECURITY

8.1 Gender and Household Food Insecurity

In the overall AFSUN survey the mean HFIAS score of 10 fell at the mid-point of a range from a low of 4.7 in Johannesburg to a high of 14.9 in Manzini, with Harare next at 14.7.[42] While there was substantial variation within the sample, food insecurity was therefore significant and widespread. Breaking down the HFIAS by household type and city provides clear evidence of the greater food insecurity in female-centred households (Table 14). In each city, the mean HFIAS score for female-centred households was higher than nuclear households, and in most cases it was higher than extended households too. In Manzini, the city with the highest HFIAS score, the figure for female-centred households was 15.6, compared to 13.4 for nuclear households. A similar difference is found in Harare, with female-centred households having the highest overall mean HFIAS score (16.1) and thus the lowest food security of any group in the sample. In cities with high overall food insecurity, female-centred households were more food insecure yet. Even in cities with relatively low food insecurity, such as Blantyre and Johannesburg, female-centred households were relatively less food secure than nuclear households.

TABLE 14: Average HFIAS Scores by Household Type and City				
	Female-Centred	Male-Centred	Nuclear	Extended	Total
Harare	16.1	14.4	14.3	14.4	14.7
Manzini	15.6	15.3	13.4	15.2	14.9
Maseru	14.1	12.4	11.9	12.0	12.8
Lusaka	12.7	9.6	11.0	11.6	11.5
Msunduzi	12.3	11.1	9.5	10.7	11.3
Cape Town	11.4	11.4	10.5	9.0	10.7
Gaborone	10.9	10.9	9.3	11.3	10.8
Maputo	10.8	9.8	9.8	10.5	10.4
Windhoek	10.6	8.8	8.5	8.7	9.3
Blantyre	7.3	3.5	5.1	4.6	5.3
Johannesburg	4.6	6.0	4.0	5.4	4.7

Similar differences were found in the second calculated food insecurity indicator, the HFIAP. In every city, without exception, a higher proportion of female-centred households than nuclear households is found in the 'severely food insecure' category (Table 15). In seven cities, female-centred households have the highest proportion of severely food insecure households of any household type, and in another three they are a close second to either extended or male-centred households. Only in the Johannesburg sample are considerably more extended and male-centred households (34%) than female-centred households (25%) severely food insecure, although Johannesburg households are the most food secure of any city in the survey.

TABLE 15: Average HFIAP Ranking by Household Type and City		Female-centred %	Nuclear %	Total %
Windhoek	Food secure	13	29	18
	Mildly food insecure	7	5	5
	Moderately food insecure	11	9	14
	Severely food insecure	69	56	63
	Total	100	100	100
Gaborone	Food secure	14	13	12
	Mildly food insecure	4	14	6
	Moderately food insecure	19	15	19
	Severely food insecure	64	58	63
	Total	100	100	100
Maseru	Food secure	3	5	5
	Mildly food insecure	4	7	6
	Moderately food insecure	27	27	25
	Severely food insecure	67	61	65
	Total	100	100	100
Manzini	Food secure	4	8	6
	Mildly food insecure	3	3	3
	Moderately food insecure	11	13	13
	Severely food insecure	82	76	79
	Total	100	100	100
Maputo	Food secure	4	10	5
	Mildly food insecure	9	8	9
	Moderately food insecure	34	30	32
	Severely food insecure	54	53	54
	Total	100	100	100
Blantyre	Food secure	22	34	34
	Mildly food insecure	12	13	14
	Moderately food insecure	26	34	30
	Severely food insecure	40	19	21
	Total	100	100	100

Lusaka	Food secure	4	5	4
	Mildly food insecure	4	4	3
	Moderately food insecure	18	22	24
	Severely food insecure	75	69	69
	Total	100	100	100
Harare	Food secure	2	2	2
	Mildly food insecure	2	2	3
	Moderately food insecure	18	25	24
	Severely food insecure	78	71	72
	Total	100	100	100
Cape Town	Food secure	14	14	15
	Mildly food insecure	4	4	5
	Moderately food insecure	11	14	12
	Severely food insecure	72	68	68
	Total	100	100	100
Msunduzi	Food secure	5	7	7
	Mildly food insecure	4	12	6
	Moderately food insecure	27	32	27
	Severely food insecure	64	49	60
	Total	100	100	100
Johannesburg	Food secure	46	46	44
	Mildly food insecure	12	14	14
	Moderately food insecure	17	16	15
	Severely food insecure	25	24	27
	Total	100	100	100
Total	Food secure	14	18	16
	Mildly food insecure	6	8	7
	Moderately food insecure	19	21	20
	Severely food insecure	62	53	57
	Total	100	100	100

The difference in the proportion of female-centred versus nuclear households that are severely food insecure is especially pronounced in Windhoek, Blantyre and Msunduzi. Although Blantyre has relatively high food security overall, this masks extreme gender-based inequality, with 40% of female-centred households in Blantyre being severely food insecure, compared to only 19% of nuclear households. The city with the highest absolute proportion of severely food insecure female-centred households is Manzini (82%). The small proportion of female-centred households in the food secure category is also lower than other household types in most cities. In seven of the eleven cities, more nuclear households than female-centred households are food secure. The figures are the same in another three. In only one (Gaborone) are there more food secure female-centred households (but only by one percentage point). Overall, 62% of female-centred households are severely food insecure, compared to 53% of nuclear households. Household type therefore appears to be a determining factor in food security status, if in different ways and to differing extent in different cities.

8.2 Gender and Dietary Diversity

The median score on the Household Dietary Diversity Scale (HDDS) for the whole sample is 5 (out of 12), with a statistically significant difference between food secure and food insecure households (i.e. correlated with HFIAP).[43] The dominant food type eaten was starch staples, with less than half the sample eating any form of animal protein. No city had any household eating from all food groups. Overall, the data suggests that poor households have a nutritionally inadequate diet, in addition to lacking a sufficient quantity of food.

There is little variation by household type, although if one group is more nutritionally disadvantaged than the others, it is male-centred households (i.e. households with no wife or female partner of the household head) (Table 16). Fully 17% of male-centred households have an HDDS score of 2 or less, compared to 14% of female-centred households and 13% of nuclear households.

HDD Score	Female-Centred %	Male-Centred %	Nuclear %	Extended %	Total %
1	3	3	2	1	2
2	11	14	11	10	11
3	11	11	10	10	10
4	12	12	11	11	11
5	14	12	13	14	14
6	12	12	13	15	13
7	12	12	12	12	12
8	10	12	10	12	10
9	7	6	7	8	7
10	4	2	6	4	4
11	2	1	3	3	2
12	3	3	3	1	2
Total	100	100	100	100	100

TABLE 16: Household Dietary Diversity by Household Type

Extended households have the lowest proportion of households with HDDS scores of 2 or less (11%). At the upper end of the dietary diversity scale, nuclear households are best off, with 12% having a score of 10 or higher. Second are female-centred households, with 9% at 10 or above, followed by extended households (8%) and male-centred households (6%). At the lower end, the percentages of households that score 5 or below on the HDDS (i.e. at or below the overall median) were 51% of female-centred households, 52% of male-centred households, 47% of nuclear households and 46% of extended households. This indicated slightly lower nutrition security in both female-centred and male-centred households relative to nuclear households, although the difference is not as stark as expected.

8.3 Gender and Adequate Food Provisioning

Food secure households, regardless of household type, have access to food most of the year (Table 17). Food insecure households, on the other hand, experience an average of four months of inadequate food provisioning. Amongst these food insecure households, female-centred households are relatively worse off in nine cities, with appreciably lower MAHFP scores than nuclear households. The exceptions are Blantyre, where female-centred food insecure households are slightly better off than nuclear food insecure households (although this amounts to only a few more days with sufficient food), and Lusaka, where there is no difference between the two household types.

TABLE 17: Months of Adequate Household Provisioning				
	Food Secure		Food Insecure	
	Female-Centred	Nuclear	Female-Centred	Nuclear
Windhoek	11.7	11.2	8.9	9.5
Gaborone	11.9	10.9	8.4	9.0
Maseru	10.9	10.8	7.1	7.8
Manzini	11.6	11.8	5.1	6.1
Maputo	10.5	11.8	8.9	9.2
Blantyre	11.3	11.4	8.8	8.6
Lusaka	11.2	10.1	9.4	9.4
Harare	11.0	11.6	6.3	7.1
Cape Town	11.1	11.4	8.3	8.9
Msunduzi	11.5	10.9	8.5	9.5
Johannesburg	11.6	11.7	8.9	9.2

Manzini and Harare are, once again, the 'hungriest' cities. In each, female-centred households are worse off still. Even when they are food insecure, nuclear households in Manzini enjoy a full month more of adequate food provisioning per year compared to female-centred food insecure households. The difference in Harare is also almost one month. Male-centred food insecure households in Manzini are the worst off of all, with fewer than five months of adequate food provisioning. Best off are female-centred food secure households in Gaborone, at almost twelve full months with enough food.

9. DETERMINANTS OF FOOD INSECURITY

Gender does not act in isolation to determine household food security, but in conjunction with other variables. This section presents a gender-based analysis of the main factors that were found to correlate significantly with food insecurity in the original analysis of the survey data as a whole, namely poverty, income, employment and education. Household size only has a weak correlation with food security and is not explored further here. The analysis that follows uses a binary classification of households into "food secure" and "food insecure" in terms of the HFIAP measure and then breaks these down further by household type.[44] The analysis sheds light not only on the causes of food insecurity, but also on how these are unequally experienced by men and women, and by members of female-centred compared to nuclear households. Although female-centred households are found to experience relative disadvantage in income, employment and education, and hence also in food security status, some of the findings suggest that female-centredness may actually mitigate some of the worst effects of poverty and that female-centred households experience less of a deficit in food security than expected.

9.1 Income, Poverty and Food Security

The survey as a whole found "a direct relationship between poverty and food insecurity", with a statistically significant correlation between food security status and both the LPI and household income.[45] The relationship between food security status and LPI was remarkably consistent across household types, clear evidence of the general poverty of the AFSUN survey sample (Table 18). In aggregate, 49% of female-centred households had LPI scores over 1.0, only slightly higher than extended (48%) and nuclear and male-centred households (both 46%). However, given that a greater proportion of female-centred households are food insecure relative to other household types, greater absolute numbers of female-centred households are in this LPI category, and "go without" food and other basic necessities more often.

TABLE 18: Food Security and Lived Poverty		Food Secure %	Food Insecure %	Total %
Female-Centred	0–1.0	91	41	51
	>1.0	9	59	49
Male-Centred	0–1.0	91	41	54
	>1.0	9	59	46
Nuclear	0–1.0	92	40	54
	>1.0	8	60	46
Extended	0–1.0	90	40	52
	>1.0	10	60	48

More revealing than the LPI is the relationship between food security and income. A strong correlation between income and food security is to be expected in urban contexts, where food is mainly purchased rather than grown. As shown above, female-centred households fall dispro-portionately into the poorest income tercile. This has clear implications for food insecurity as "food security increases with a rise in household income across all household types, and this relationship is statistically sig-nificant."[46] Women's lower income does appear to translate into lower food security for female-centred households. However, the relationship is not a simple one. Analysis by household type suggests an important role for gender in mediating the relationship between low income and food insecurity (Table 19).

Amongst food secure female-centred households, 23% fall within the poorest income tercile. This was a higher proportion of 'food secure yet poor' households than any other household type. Amongst nuclear house-holds that were food secure, for example, only 13% are within the poor-est income tercile. Amongst food insecure households, 30% of nuclear households and 41% of extended households are in the "least poor" income tercile, compared with only 22% of female-centred households. In other words, higher household income does not appear to guarantee food security, nor does lower income necessarily mean food insecurity. While female-centred households are still more likely to be both income-poor and food insecure, the evidence suggests that the relationship between food security and income varies in nature and strength between household types. For a certain sub-category of households, food security is attained despite income poverty, and that is more the case for female-centred households. This is consistent with findings from other African contexts demonstrating that "the female gender of the head compensates for the difference in income *at low levels of income*" (italics in original).[47]

TABLE 19: Food Security and Household Income		Food Secure %	Food Insecure %
Female-Centred	Poorest	23	45
	Less poor	30	33
	Least poor	47	22
Male-Centred	Poorest	18	38
	Less poor	35	37
	Least poor	48	25
Nuclear	Poorest	13	31
	Less poor	25	39
	Least poor	62	30
Extended	Poorest	10	25
	Less poor	21	33
	Least poor	70	41

The overall survey data also demonstrated a correlation between food security and waged employment specifically as a source of income. Although weak, the relationship is statistically significant.[48] Across all household types, food insecure households report lower access to wage income and higher dependence on casual work relative to food secure households. Given this correlation, the higher rate of unemployment and lower rate of waged employment in female-centred households would be expected to correlate directly with their higher food insecurity. The picture in reality is more complex (Table 20). Amongst food secure households, only 57% of those that are female-centred have access to income from waged employment, compared to 70% of food secure male-centred households, 72% of food secure nuclear households and 67% of food secure extended households. Nor was this made up for by casual work or informal business: amongst food secure households, the proportion of female-centred households with such income was lower than nuclear households. Amongst food insecure households, more nuclear households than female-centred households again reported income from wage work and casual employment, although female-centred food insecure households were more likely to earn income from informal business. Thus, as was the case for income, it appears that some female-centred households manage to attain food security despite their more precarious employment status and that relatively more nuclear households remain food insecure despite earning income from waged employment.

TABLE 20: Food Security and Source of Income				
		Food Secure % of HH	Food Insecure % of HH	Total % of HH
Female-Centred	Wage work	57	38	42
	Casual work	15	27	25
	Remittances	18	15	15
	Urban and rural agriculture	3	3	3
	Formal business	3	3	3
	Informal business	19	23	22
	Social grants	32	32	32
Male-Centred	Wage work	70	50	54
	Casual work	13	25	22
	Remittances	11	9	9
	Urban/rural agriculture	5	1	2
	Formal business	5	2	3
	Informal business	13	16	15
	Social grants	6	13	11
Nuclear	Wage work	72	55	59
	Casual work	17	32	28
	Remittances	9	10	9
	Urban/rural agriculture	5	3	4
	Formal business	5	3	4
	Informal business	21	20	20
	Social grants	15	16	16
Extended	Wage work	67	60	61
	Casual work	18	24	23
	Remittances	9	13	12
	Urban/rural agriculture	7	7	7
	Formal business	10	6	7
	Informal business	26	27	27
	Social grants	18	19	19

Remittances and social grants are especially important to female-centred households. Eighteen percent of food secure and 15% of food insecure female-centred households received remittances (higher than all other household types and levels of food security). The source of these remittances is unknown but they probably come from partners or adult children working in other cities or countries. Remittances may thus well be decisive in purchasing food in households that might otherwise be food insecure. A sizable proportion of both food secure and insecure female-centred households also derive income from social grants (32% in each category). Social grants are provided to support children, the elderly and the disabled. As women are typically responsible for providing care, the allocation of social grants is highly gendered (as well as being concentrated in the three South African cities of Cape Town, Johannesburg and Msunduzi). Given the significance of social grants for female-centred households, even those that are food secure, the removal of grants would have the effect of creating larger numbers of food insecure households and further widening the gender gap in patterns of urban hunger and poverty.

9.2 Education and Food Insecurity

Education is related to food security in a number of ways. Firstly, it has a positive effect on employment and income, which in turn are essential determinants of food security in an urban setting. Secondly, the education of women in particular is broadly recognized as an important contributor to household food security.[49] The overall AFSUN findings demonstrate an association between education and food security that was statistically significant both at the regional level and for individual cities (albeit with weaker strength in the poorer cities). Across all household types, lower education of the household head is indeed associated with household food insecurity, with levels of food insecurity falling with increased education (Table 21).

TABLE 21: Education Level of Household Heads and Household Food Security Status		Food Secure %	Food Insecure %
Female-Centred Households	No formal schooling	12	88
	Primary school	12	88
	High school	23	77
	Tertiary education	45	55
Male-Centred Households	No formal schooling	6	94
	Primary school	14	86
	High school	27	73
	Tertiary education	52	48
Nuclear Households	No formal schooling	11	89
	Primary school	19	81
	High school	27	73
	Tertiary education	54	46
Extended Households	No formal schooling	11	89
	Primary school	20	80
	High school	24	76
	Tertiary education	50	50

Not only are the heads of female-centred households likely to have lower levels of education, but the 'education advantage' for female-centred households appears less strong than it is for other household types. Amongst female-centred households whose heads have a tertiary education, 55% are nevertheless food insecure. The equivalent figure for nuclear households is 46% – still alarmingly high, but considerably lower than female-centred households. For households whose heads have no formal schooling, regardless of household type, there is a predictable association with food insecurity, at close to 90%. But for households that are not female-centred, the proportion that are food insecure drops significantly for each additional level of education. For female-centred households, by contrast, there appears to be virtually no food security enhancement associated with primary education, and the decline in food insecurity with each additional level of education is less than the equivalent for nuclear households in particular.

The reasons for this disparity could include various intersections between gender, labour and income, such as fewer opportunities for women in the labour market, limited alternative livelihood opportunities, and lower pay for women across education and employment levels. An important additional factor is that household heads of female-centred households, especially those with few or no other adult members, have no partner with whom to practise a household division of labour between domestic tasks and income-earning activities. The same is true of male-centred households, but they have fewer child and other dependants to care and provide for. These associations amongst education, employment, income, gender and household type warrant further analysis, including separate analyses for individual cities as well as more sophisticated statistical treatment to determine significant multivariate relationships. What the findings suggest, however, is that the correlation between education and food security is weaker not only in the poorer cities, but also, and probably for similar reasons, for female-centred households.

9.3 Food Sources and Food Insecurity

The AFSUN survey found two primary statistically significant relationships between food security and food sources. The first was with supermarket use, with greater numbers of food secure households using supermarkets. The fact that more female-centred households used supermarkets, despite more of them being food insecure, warrants further interrogation of the data. This anomaly could simply be a statistical artifact in the data set as a whole, with uneven distribution of female-centred households amongst the eleven cities, and more female-centred households in those cities where supermarket use is more prevalent. Secondly, there is the higher incidence of social grants and food transfers in food insecure households. As discussed above, grants are received by a higher proportion of female-centred households in most, but not all, cities. Their need for such transfers likely relates to their food insecurity, but food transfers also provide a plausible explanation for the fact that they are not even more food insecure, given their relatively weaker income, employment and education status.

Urban agriculture did not show a statistically significant correlation with food security status. This is consistent with findings in other studies, that the prevalence of urban agriculture in poor urban communities has been greatly exaggerated and is as much entrepreneurial as survivalist.[50] Although the overall proportion of households practising urban agriculture was low, more nuclear and extended households than either male- or female-centred households engage in it. This suggests that it may be shortages of labour, resources and time that constrain female-centred households from supplementing household food provision in this way. Follow-up studies are needed to explore the household dynamics of urban agriculture in order to identify such constraints and how they are experienced by different types of households in different cities.

10. CONCLUSIONS AND POLICY POINTERS

As this analysis has shown, there does appear to be a link between gender and food insecurity in the eleven cities surveyed by AFSUN. This is evident in the higher levels of food insecurity amongst female-centred households (defined as having a female head and no husband/male partner in the household, but including children, other relatives or friends). In the sample as a whole, 77% of all households were either moderately or severely food insecure. Amongst female-centred households the proportion was 81%, while for nuclear households it was 74%. This aggregation masks a high level of variation amongst the eleven cities. Even some cities that appear more food secure, such as Blantyre, have significantly higher food insecurity amongst female-centred households. In cities such as Harare and Manzini, relative gender parity exists but only because of extremely high overall food insecurity. Chronic food insecurity is thus pervasive amongst the urban poor in Southern Africa, but female-centred households suffer disproportionately from both poverty and related food insecurity.

The key findings to emerge from this gender analysis of the AFSUN data are the following:

- In terms of HFIAP rankings, four out of five female-centred households are food insecure, compared to three out of four nuclear households.

- Female-centred households score worse on other food security indicators, including dietary diversity and months of adequate household food provisioning.

- Food insecurity of female-centred households is related to the greater poverty of these households, which are characterized by lower income and more precarious employment and livelihoods.

- Some female-centred households nevertheless manage to attain food security despite lower income.

- Social transfers (and especially formal social grants) are especially important for female-centred households in countries and cities where they are available.

- The effect of education in enhancing food security is weaker for female-centred households than for other household types.

By comparing female-centred and nuclear households, light is shed both on the determinants of urban food insecurity – which relate fundamentally to income, employment and education – and on the manifest gender inequalities in access to the largely income-based entitlements to food in the city. What it also shows, however, is the entrenched and systemic nature of gender discrimination and inequality, and thus the lack of any quick fixes, such as the much-touted "education for girls" strategy, as a panacea for poverty and hunger.[51] Education alone, in the absence of more fundamental social change, is evidently not sufficient to lift female-centred households out of poverty and hunger, as long as labour market discrimination, unequal access to capital and resources, and culturally embedded expectations of women's responsibility for caring and reproductive labour remain in place.

These insights can be used to design and implement practical and strategic interventions that could simultaneously and synergistically address both gender inequality and food insecurity.[52] Practically, and in the immediate term, interventions such as social grants and food aid, if targeted at the poorest households, will automatically capture a greater proportion of female-centred households. More strategically, the aim should be to make female-centred households less poor, and thus more food secure. Enhancing food security for the urban poor requires education and training, job creation, and income generation strategies, ensuring equitable access to such opportunities for women and girls. Supporting and enabling women's engagement in such activities and enterprises – including in food production and marketing – has the potential to strengthen food security at the same time as reducing gender inequality, in a form of virtuous cycle.

These findings have implications for urban, national and regional policy interventions aimed at reducing urban food insecurity. Gender analysis of the AFSUN survey findings demonstrates the importance of gender and household type in understanding the determinants of food insecurity, and can provide the basis for designing and implementing effective strategies for food security enhancement. The AFSUN data also provide a baseline against which the effects of policy changes and other interventions aimed at addressing food insecurity, including their gender impacts, can be measured and monitored.

ENDNOTES

1   UN-HABITAT, *The State of African Cities, 2010: Governance, Inequality and Urban Land Markets* (Nairobi: UN-HABITAT, 2010).

2   J. Crush and B. Frayne, *The Invisible Crisis: Urban Food Insecurity in Southern Africa*, AFSUN Urban Food Security Series No. 1, Cape Town and Kingston, 2009.

3   A. Sen, *Poverty and Famines: An Essay on Entitlement and Deprivation* (Oxford, Clarendon, 1981).

4   Crush and Frayne, *Invisible Crisis*.

5   B. Frayne et al., *The State of Urban Food Insecurity in Southern Africa*, AFSUN Urban Food Security Series No. 2, Cape Town and Kingston, 2010; B. Frayne, J. Battersby-Lennard, R. Fincham and G. Haysom, *Urban Food Security in South Africa: Case Study of Cape Town, Msunduzi and Johannesburg*. Development Planning Division Working Paper Series No. 15, DBSA, Midrand, 2009.

6   See AFSUN Urban Food Security Series Nos. 3 to 9 at www.afsun.org

7   Sen, *Poverty and Famines*.

8   Frayne et al., *State of Urban Food Insecurity in Southern Africa*, p. 7.

9   L. Patel and T. Hochfeld, "It Buys Food But Does It Change Gender Relations? Child Support Grants in Soweto, South Africa" *Gender and Development* 19(2) (2011): 229-40; E. Kimani-Murage, P. Holding, J-C. Fotso, A. Ezeh, N. Madise, E. Kahurani and E. Zulu, "Food Security and Nutritional Outcomes among Urban Poor Orphans in Nairobi, Kenya" *Journal of Urban Health* 88(S2) (2011): 282-97; L. Patel, "Poverty, Gender and Social Protection: Child Support Grants in Soweto, South Africa" *Journal of Policy Practice* 11(1-2) (2012): 106-20.

10   S. Atkinson, "Approaches and Actors in Urban Food Security in Developing Countries" *Habitat International* 19(2) (1995): 151-63.

11   A. Quisumbing, L. Brown, H. Feldstein, L. Haddad and C. Peña, *Women: The Key to Food Security* (Washington, D.C.: International Food Policy Research

Institute, 1995); M. Vaughan, *The Story of an African Famine* (Cambridge; Cambridge University Press, 1987); C. Moser, *Gender Planning and Development: Theory, Practice, and Training* (London: Routledge, 1993); N. Kabeer, *Reversed Realities in Development Thought* (London and New York: Verso, 1994); B. Agarwal, "'Bargaining' and Gender Relations: Within and Beyond the Household" *Feminist Economics* 3(1) (1997): 1-51.

12   E. Kennedy and P. Peters, "Household Food Security and Child Nutrition: The Interaction of Income and Gender of Household Head" *World Development* 20(8) (1992): 1077-85.

13   V. Reddy and R. Moletsane, "The Gendered Dimensions of Food Security in South Africa: A Review of the Literature" Gender and Development Unit, Human Sciences Research Council, Pretoria, 2009.

14   I. Tinker, *Street Foods: Urban Food and Employment in Developing Countries* (Oxford and New York: Oxford University Press, 1997); C. Levin, M. Ruel, S. Morris, D. Maxwell, M. Armar-Klemesu and C. Ahiadeke, "Working Women in an Urban Setting: Traders, Vendors and Food Security in Accra" *World Development* 27(11) (1999): 1977-91; G. Porter, F. Lyon and D. Potts, "Market Institutions and Urban Food Supply in West and Southern Africa: A Review" *Progress in Development Studies* 7(2) (2007): 115-34.

15   D. Drakakis-Smith, T. Bowyer-Bower and D. Tevera, "Urban Poverty and Urban Agriculture: An Overview of Linkages in Harare" *Habitat International* 19(2) (1995): 183-93; A. Hovorka, "Urban Agriculture: Addressing Practical and Strategic Gender Needs" *Development in Practice* 16(1) (2006): 51-61; L. Mougeot (ed.), *Agropolis: The Social, Political and Environmental Dimensions of Urban Agriculture* (Ottawa: IDRC, 2005).

16   J. Bongaarts, "Household Size and Composition in the Developing World in the 1990s" *Population Studies: A Journal of Demography* 55(3) (2001): 263-79; D. Posel, "Who Are the Heads of Household, What Do They Do, and Is the Concept of Headship Useful? An Analysis of Headship in South Africa" *Development Southern Africa* 18(5) (2001): 651-70; S. Mathis, "Disobedient Daughters? Changing Women's Roles in Rural Households in KwaZulu-Natal" *Journal of Southern African Studies* 37(4) (2011): 831-48.

17   S. Chant, "Re-thinking the 'Feminisation of Poverty' in Relation to Aggregate Gender Indices" *Journal of Human Development* 7(2) (2006): 201-20.

18   S. Lemke, "Empowered Women and the Need to Empower Men: Gender Relations and Food Security in Black South African Households" *Studies of Tribes and Tribals* 1(1) (2003): 59-67; B. Dodson with H. Simelane, D. Tevera, T. Green, A. Chikanda and F. de Vletter, *Gender, Migration and Remittances in Southern Africa*, SAMP Migration Policy Series No. 49, Cape Town and Kingston, 2008; E. Dungumaro, "Gender Differentials in Household Structure and Socioeconomic Characteristics in South Africa" *Journal of Comparative Family Studies* 39(4) (2008): 429–51; A. Goebel, B. Dodson and T. Hill, "Urban Advantage or Urban Penalty? A Case Study of Female-Headed Households in a South African City" *Health and Place* 16(3) (2010): 573-80.

19   Levin et al., "Working Women in an Urban Setting."

20   Frayne et al., *State of Urban Food Insecurity in Southern Africa*.

21   Quisimbing et al., *Women: The Key to Food Security*; Agarwal, "'Bargaining' and Gender Relations"; L. Haddad, J. Hoddinott and H. Alderman, eds., *Intrahousehold*

Resource Allocation in Developing Countries: Methods, Models, and Policy (Baltimore: Johns Hopkins University Press and IFPRI, 1997).

22   Frayne et al., *State of Urban Food Insecurity in Southern Africa*.

23   Ibid.

24   This means that inter-city comparisons, while illustrative, are not of strictly statistically equivalent representative sample populations.

25   The normal binary household typology of female- or male-headed was replaced in the AFSUN survey with a four-fold typology: female-centred households are those with no husband/male partner in the household but can include relatives, children, and friends; male-centred households have no wife/female partner in the household but can include relatives, children, and friends; nuclear households have a husband/male partner and a wife/female partner with or without children; and extended families have a husband/male partner and a wife/female partner and children and relatives.

26   Zimbabwe was in a state of acute political and economic crisis at the time of the survey, marked by hyperinflation and food shortages; see G.Tawodzera, L. Zanamwe and J. Crush, *The State of Food Insecurity in Harare, Zimbabwe*, AFSUN Urban Food Security Series No. 13, Cape Town and Kingston, 2012.

27   Frayne et al., *The State of Urban Food Insecurity in Southern Africa*, p. 25.

28   J. Coates, A. Swindale and P. Bilinsky, "Household Food Insecurity Access Scale (HFIAS) for Measurement of Food Access: Indicator Guide (Version 3)" Food and Nutrition Technical Assistance Project, Academy for Educational Development, Washington, D.C., 2007, p.18.

29   Ibid., pp. 21-2.

30   A. Swindale and P. Bilinsky, "Household Dietary Diversity Score (HDDS) for Measurement of Household Food Access: Indicator Guide (Version 2)" Food and Nutrition Technical Assistance Project, Academy for Educational Development, Washington, D.C., 2006.

31   P. Bilinsky and A. Swindale, "Months of Adequate Household Food Provisioning (MAHFP) for Measurement of Household Food Access: Indicator Guide" Food and Nutrition Technical Assistance Project, Academy for Educational Development, Washington, D.C., 2007.

32   This is probably because the sample was drawn from an area of the city in which urban agriculture is extensively practised, unlike most of Blantyre's poor residential neighbourhoods.

33   Frayne et al, *State of Urban Food Insecurity in Southern Africa*, p. 34.

34   Ibid, p. 49.

35   O. Kuku, C. Gunderson and S. Garasky, "Differences in Food Insecurity between Adults and Children in Zimbabwe" *Food Policy* 36(2011): 311-17.

36   Frayne et al., *State of Urban Food Insecurity in Southern Africa*.

37   M. Ruel, C. Levin, M. Armar-Klemesu and D. Maxwell, "Good Care Practices Can Mitigate the Negative Effects of Poverty and Low Maternal Schooling on Children's Nutritional Status: Evidence from Accra" *World Development* 27 (1999): 1993-2009.

38   Afrobarometer, "Lived Poverty in Africa: Desperation, Hope and Patience" Briefing Paper No. 11, Cape Town, 2004.

39   Patel, "Poverty, Gender and Social Protection."

40   J. Crush and B. Frayne, "Supermarket Expansion and the Informal Food Economy in Southern African Cities: Implications for Urban Food Security" *Journal of Southern African Studies* 37(4) (2011): 781-807.

41   Frayne et al., *State of Urban Food Insecurity in Southern Africa*, p. 25.

42   Ibid.

43   Ibid.

44   HFIAP categories "food secure" and "mildly food insecure" are grouped together as food secure households. "Moderately" and "severely" food insecure categories are grouped into a single "food insecure" category.

45   Ibid., p. 34. LPI scores of <1 indicate never/seldom without. Scores >1 indicate increasingly greater degrees of deprivation.

46   Ibid., p. 37.

47   Kennedy and Peters, "Household Food Security and Child Nutrition."

48   Frayne et al., *State of Urban Food Insecurity in Southern Africa*.

49   Ruel et al., "Good Care Practices."

50   A. Hovorka, "Entrepreneurial Opportunities in Botswana: (Re)shaping Urban Agriculture Discourse" *Journal of Contemporary African Studies* 22(3) (2004): 367-88. J. Crush, A. Hovorka and D. Tevera, *Urban Food Production and Household Food Security in Southern African Cities*, AFSUN Urban Food Security Series No. 4, Cape Town and Kingston, 2010.

51   B. Herz and G. Sperling, "What Works in Girls' Education: Evidence and Policies from the Developing World" (Washington, D.C.: Council on Foreign Relations, 2004).

52   Moser, *Gender Planning and Development*.

Printed in the United States
By Bookmasters